MATH
CLASS

A COMPANION QUIZ BOOK

TABLE OF CONTENTS

ARE YOU SMARTER THAN A 5TH GRADER

Welcome to *Are You Smarter Than a 5th Grader*! The show that gives grown-ups the chance to win $100,000 by testing their smarts and proving that they are smarter than a 5th grader.

To play, each contestant faces different subjects, starting with the 1st-Grade level and going all the way to the 5th-Grade level. Before each grade level begins, the contestant chooses one of their classmates to help.

The questions are taken straight from grade-school textbooks, randomly mixed among open-ended, multiple-choice, and true/false questions.

> 1st–2nd Grade: 1 question each
> 3rd–4th Grade: 2 questions each
>
> In 1st–4th Grade, the contestant receives 2 cheats: COPY and PEEK.

- If a contestant chooses to COPY, they use their classmate's answer, sight unseen.

- If a contestant chooses to PEEK, they are shown their classmate's answer and can choose to use that answer or not.

- If the contestant gets a question right, they earn the money at stake and move up the ladder. But if they get a question wrong, they stay at their current level, and continue on with their questions!

After all 1st- through 4th-Grade questions are asked, it's time for the 5th-Grade questions . . . and the chance to multiply the money a contestant has already won!

5th Grade: 5 questions to answer with 60 seconds on the clock. The right answers won't be revealed until all 5 answers are locked in!

- The money is multiplied 2×, 3×, 4×, 5×, 10× with each correct answer.

- If a contestant isn't confident with their answer, they have one cheat available to them. This is played just like a PEEK, where the contestant can go with their classmate's answer or choose one of their own, at which point we'll see if they are correct or not.

Now it's your turn to test your smarts! Turn the page and find out if you're smarter than a 5th grader!

$10,000

$5,000

$2,500

$1,000

$500

$250

MEET THE CLASSMATES

SAYA

FAVORITE SUBJECTS
- Vocabulary
- History

SKILLS / FACTS
- Contortionist
- Detailed character artist
- Speaks fluent Japanese

PATRICK

FAVORITE SUBJECTS
- Vocabulary
- Grammar

SKILLS / FACTS
- Fascinated by dinosaurs
- Plays the trumpet
- Kung Fu master

COLIN

FAVORITE SUBJECTS
- Social Studies
- Anatomy

SKILLS / FACTS
- Boxer
- Pinewood Derby car champ
- Champion swimmer

MIA

FAVORITE SUBJECTS
- Science
- English

SKILLS / FACTS
- Published poet
- Plays the harp
- Runs cross-country

TRISTAN

FAVORITE SUBJECTS
- History
- Math

SKILLS / FACTS
- Tae Kwon Do master
- Has pet bearded dragons
- Created a rap song about the show

COOPER

FAVORITE SUBJECTS
- Math
- Health

SKILLS / FACTS
- President of his class
- Juggler
- Push-up pro

AMIRA

FAVORITE SUBJECTS
- Reading
- Science

SKILLS / FACTS
- Wants to find life outside of Earth
- Wants to work for NASA
- Honor roll student

QUINNE

FAVORITE SUBJECTS
- Vocabulary
- Reading

SKILLS / FACTS
- Wants to be a roller coaster engineer
- Built a skate ramp in her yard
- Drummer in a band

JAMIR

FAVORITE SUBJECTS
- Grammar
- Science

SKILLS / FACTS
- Aspiring action star
- Has a funny nickname
- Bow tie fanatic

CHLOE

FAVORITE SUBJECTS
- Literature
- Math

SKILLS / FACTS
- Does stand-up comedy
- MMA champ
- Speaks Mandarin

NICK

FAVORITE SUBJECTS
- History
- Geography

SKILLS / FACTS
- Loves game shows
- Kayaker
- Hip-Hop dancer

ISABELLA

FAVORITE SUBJECTS
- Reading
- History

SKILLS / FACTS
- Salsa dancer
- Has won multiple pageants
- Loves sloths

FIRST GRADE

1 NICK IS WEIGHING OBJECTS ON A BALANCE SCALE. IF TRAY 1 IS LOWER THAN TRAY 2, WHICH TRAY IS HOLDING AN OBJECT WITH MORE WEIGHT?

2 WHAT'S THE SUM OF THE DIGITS IN THE NUMBER 246?

3 WHAT LETTER IN THE ALPHABET CAN REPRESENT THE MULTIPLICATION SYMBOL?

4 IF COLIN NAMED EVERY NUMBER UNDER 100 THAT ENDED IN THE SUFFIX "-TEEN," HOW MANY NUMBERS WOULD HE HAVE NAMED?

5 TRUE OR FALSE? USING CURRENT US COINS, THE ONLY WAY TO MAKE 11 CENTS IS TO HAVE 1 DIME AND 1 PENNY.

6

IF SAYA MAKES A DOZEN WATER BALLOONS AND DROPS 4 OF THEM ON PATRICK, WHAT IS THE TOTAL NUMBER OF WATER BALLOONS THAT SHE HAS LEFT?
  A. 6   B. 8   C. 10

7

WHICH OF THE FOLLOWING WILL GIVE YOU THE SAME ANSWER AS 6 + 2?
  A. 4 + 1   B. 5 + 3   C. 7 + 0

8

TRISTAN ARRANGES ALL HIS BOOKS ON 4 SHELVES. IF THERE ARE EXACTLY 10 BOOKS ON EACH SHELF, WHAT IS THE TOTAL NUMBER OF BOOKS HE HAS?

9

COUNTING BY FIVES, WHAT'S THE FIFTH NUMBER AFTER 5?

10

IF MIA ADDS UP ALL THE SIDES IN A TRIANGLE, A SQUARE, AND A RECTANGLE, HOW MANY SIDES ARE THERE IN TOTAL?
  A. 10   B. 11   C. 12

11

IF CHLOE MAKES A DOZEN CUPCAKES AND PATRICK EATS 5 OF THEM, HOW MANY CUPCAKES ARE LEFT?

12

QUINNE LOOKS AT HER CALENDAR AND SEES THAT TODAY IS SUNDAY THE 15TH. WHAT WILL BE THE DATE OF THE FOLLOWING SATURDAY?

SECOND GRADE

1 NICK NEEDS TO BE 4 FEET TALL TO RIDE THE ROLLER COASTER. HE IS ONLY 3 FEET 3 INCHES TALL. HOW MUCH TALLER DOES HE NEED TO BE TO RIDE?

2 TRUE OR FALSE? IF COLIN MULTIPLIES AN EVEN NUMBER BY AN ODD NUMBER, THE RESULT WILL ALWAYS BE EVEN.

3 BY DEFINITION, AN OCTAGON HAS HOW MANY MORE SIDES THAN A HEXAGON?

4 HOW MANY EVEN NUMBERS ARE THERE BETWEEN 21 AND 33?

5 WHAT IS THE PERIMETER OF A REGULAR HEXAGON WITH 5-INCH SIDES?

6 IF ISABELLA PUT A $1 BILL IN A MACHINE TO BUY A 60-CENT SNACK, HOW MUCH CHANGE SHOULD SHE RECEIVE?

    A. 1 QUARTER AND 2 DIMES

    B. 2 DIMES AND 3 NICKELS

    C. 3 DIMES AND 2 NICKELS

7

IT TAKES COOPER 75 MINUTES TO DO HIS HOMEWORK. IF HE BEGINS AT 7:00 P.M., HOW MUCH TIME WILL HE HAVE LEFT TO PRACTICE HIS DANCE MOVES BEFORE 10:00 P.M. BEDTIME?

8

HOW MANY FEET ARE IN 48 INCHES?

9

THE EQUATION 1 + 2 = 3 FEATURES HOW MANY ADDENDS?

10

JAMIR HAS 15 EARTHWORMS. MIA HAS 20 MORE EARTHWORMS THAN JAMIR. WHAT IS THE NUMBER OF EARTHWORMS THEY HAVE COMBINED?
A. 35   B. 50   C. 65

11

HOW MANY ENDPOINTS DOES A LINE SEGMENT HAVE?

12

IF YOU WROTE OUT ALL THE WHOLE NUMBERS FROM 1 TO 99, HOW MANY ZEROS WOULD YOU USE?

THIRD GRADE

1 WHICH IS WARMER? 40 DEGREES FAHRENHEIT OR 20 DEGREES CELSIUS?

2 TRUE OR FALSE? WHEN ADDING TOGETHER 2 TWO-DIGIT INTEGERS, THE SUM CAN NEVER BE A FOUR-DIGIT INTEGER.

3 IF TRISTAN RECEIVES A WEEKLY ALLOWANCE OF $2.50, HOW MANY WEEKS WOULD HE HAVE TO SAVE UP ALL HIS MONEY IN ORDER TO BUY A $100 SKATEBOARD?

4 SAYA HAS GROWN 3 INCHES TALLER EVERY YEAR FOR THE PAST 5 YEARS. IF SHE IS NOW 4 FEET 3 INCHES TALL, HOW TALL WAS SHE 5 YEARS AGO?

5 WHICH OF THE FOLLOWING IS A MIXED NUMBER?
A. ¾   B. 55.11   C. 1½

6 AMIRA'S 5TH-GRADE CLASS ORDERED 20 CHEESEBURGERS. EACH OF THEM WAS $1.90 INCLUDING TAX. HOW MUCH DID THE BILL COME TO?

7 PATRICK AND ISABELLA START RIDING THEIR BIKES FROM THE SAME POINT. IF PATRICK RIDES WEST FOR 2 MILES AND ISABELLA RIDES EAST FOR 7 MILES, HOW MANY MILES APART ARE PATRICK AND ISABELLA?

8 COLIN HAS $8 TO SPEND AT THE SNACK BAR. IF HE SPENDS ½ OF THE MONEY ON POPCORN AND ¼ OF THE MONEY ON SODA, HOW MUCH MONEY DOES HE HAVE LEFT?

9 WHICH OF THE FOLLOWING IS EQUAL TO 1 ACRE?
A. 4,356 SQUARE FEET
B. 43,560 SQUARE FEET
C. 435,600 SQUARE FEET

10 TRUE OR FALSE? ALL ODD NUMBERS ARE PRIME NUMBERS.

11 IF MR. DOE GIVES ⅓ OF HIS SALARY TO HIS MORTGAGE, ⅙ TO CHARITY, AND ½ TO HIS WIFE, HOW MUCH DOES HE HAVE LEFT TO SPEND ON NEW FISHING GEAR?

12 TRUE OR FALSE? A TOOTHPICK 6 CENTIMETERS LONG IS SHORTER THAN A KEY THAT IS 3 INCHES LONG.

13

FOURTH GRADE

1 IF YOU INVITED 32 FRIENDS TO YOUR BIRTHDAY PARTY AND WANTED TO SERVE EACH ONE A CUP OF MILK, HOW MANY GALLONS WOULD YOU NEED?

2 TRUE OR FALSE? $5/5$ IS AN IMPROPER FRACTION.

3 COOPER CAN MAKE 3 MODEL AIRPLANES IN 4 HOURS. AT THAT RATE, HOW LONG WILL IT TAKE HIM TO MAKE 5 MODEL AIRPLANES?

4 100 DEGREES CELSIUS IS WHAT TEMPERATURE IN FAHRENHEIT?

5 IF A PEACH PIT IS $1/6$ THE WEIGHT OF A PEACH AND YOU HAVE 24 POUNDS OF PEACHES, HOW MANY TOTAL POUNDS ARE THE PITS?

6 A NONAGON IS A SHAPE WITH HOW MANY SIDES?

7

IF THE MATH CLASS CONSTRUCTS A TOWER OUT OF 24 LUNCH SANDWICHES, 3 OF WHICH HAVE BOLOGNA, WHAT PERCENTAGE OF THE SANDWICHES HAVE BOLOGNA?

8

WHAT IS THE MEDIAN IN THE FOLLOWING SET OF NUMBERS? (4, 6, 8, 10, 12)

9

WHAT IS 388 ROUNDED TO THE NEAREST THOUSAND?

10

TWO FORTNIGHTS IS EQUIVALENT TO HOW MANY WEEKS?

11

WHAT IS THE SIDE LENGTH OF A SQUARE WITH AN AREA OF 64?

12

IF YOU SUBTRACT THE ROMAN NUMERAL LXX FROM THE ROMAN NUMERAL XC, WHAT ROMAN NUMERAL IS THE ANSWER?

FIFTH

1 WHAT IS THE SMALLEST COMPOSITE NUMBER?

2 THE FRACTION ¹²/₃₀ IS EQUIVALENT TO WHAT PERCENT?

3 WHAT IS THE GREATEST COMMON DIVISOR OF 160 AND 200?

4 NICK SPENDS 20% OF HIS ALLOWANCE ON CANDY. IF HE BUYS $1.50 WORTH OF CANDY, HOW MUCH IS HIS ALLOWANCE?

5 HOW MANY SQUARE METERS ARE IN 1 HECTARE?

6 A VENN DIAGRAM IS COMPOSED OF A MINIMUM OF HOW MANY CIRCLES?

7

HOW MANY COMPOSITE NUMBERS ARE THERE FROM 1 THROUGH 10?

8

IF A CAR IS TRAVELING 120 MILES PER HOUR, HOW MANY FEET PER MINUTE IS IT TRAVELING?

9

THE VALUE OF PI TO TWO DECIMAL PLACES IS 3.14. IF SAYA CONTINUES WRITING OUT PI, WHAT NUMBER COMES NEXT, IN THE THIRD DECIMAL POSITION?

10

AMIRA HAS A BOX OF 35 RED AND GREEN CANDLES. IF THE RATIO OF RED TO GREEN IS 3 TO 4, HOW MANY GREEN CANDLES ARE THERE?

11

WHAT NUMBER EQUALS 10 TO THE FOURTH POWER?

12

HOW MANY ACRES ARE IN 1 SQUARE MILE?

$$30°$$

$$g(x)=\sqrt{x(x-a)(x-b)}$$

$$15$$

$$60°$$

$$\frac{x^2+y^2}{a^2}+\frac{z^2}{b^2}=$$

$$\pi=3.1495 93\ldots$$

$$x=\sqrt{\frac{b^2}{c}+c-\frac{b}{2}}$$

$$x^2-3^2-4^2=0$$

$$x=?$$

$$x=\frac{-b\pm\sqrt{b^2-4ac}}{2a}$$

$$y$$

$$y)$$

$$\pi=3.14$$

FIRST GRADE

1 Starting with 1, what is the sum of the first 5 counting numbers?

2 If Jamir's dog, Pete, is 14 dog years old, and 1 human year equals 7 dog years, how many human years old is Pete?

3 Is the following equation true or false? 14 < 15

SECOND GRADE

4 **TRUE OR FALSE?** When you subtract a two-digit integer from another two-digit integer, the result is always a single-digit integer.

5 Chloe makes a map of her school that has a scale of 1 inch = 50 feet. If it is 150 feet from the gym to the library, how many inches is that on her map?
a. 2   b. 3   c. 4

THIRD GRADE

6 3½ yards is equivalent to how many inches?

7 If Cooper has ten dozen video games, how many scores of video games does he have?

8 25 divided by 5 is equal to 2 multiplied by what number?

9 A rectangle with a width of 5 and a length of 3 has how many lines of symmetry?

FOURTH GRADE

11 On the coordinate plane, what is the x-coordinate of the origin?

10 If you take the square root of 169 and the square root of 49 and add those numbers together, what's the result?

12 What is the sum of ⅔ and ¹⁄₁₁ in its simplest form?

FIFTH GRADE

14 What's the volume, in cubic centimeters, of a cube with a surface area of 96 centimeters squared?

13 How many square yards are equivalent to 1 acre?

15 What is the cubed root of 8?

FIRST GRADE

1 WHAT IS THE LOWEST TWO-DIGIT COUNTING NUMBER?

2 WHAT FUNCTION IN MATH IS THE OPPOSITE OF SUBTRACTION?

3 MIA HAS A QUARTER. NICK HAS 1 DIME, 2 NICKELS, AND A PENNY. WHO HAS MORE MONEY?

SECOND GRADE

4 IN A LEAP YEAR, THE 365TH DAY OF THE YEAR FALLS ON WHAT DATE?

5 IF IT IS 4:37 P.M. ON A STANDARD CLOCK, HOW MANY TOTAL MINUTES WILL PASS UNTIL THE NEXT TIME THE MINUTE HAND IS EXACTLY ON THE 6?

6 WHAT IS THE LARGEST THREE-DIGIT WHOLE NUMBER THAT CONTAINS THE DIGITS 3, 9, AND 2?

THIRD GRADE

7 TRUE OR FALSE? 1 SQUARE KILOMETER IS LARGER IN AREA THAN 1 SQUARE MILE.

8 COMPLETE THE FOLLOWING ANALOGY: "PENTAGON" IS TO "5" AS "HEPTAGON" IS TO WHAT NUMBER?

9 IF CHLOE HAS A POUND AND A HALF OF POPCORN AND SHE'S PUTTING IT INTO 1-OUNCE BOWLS, WHAT IS THE TOTAL NUMBER OF BOWLS SHE NEEDS TO FILL IN ORDER TO USE ALL THE POPCORN?

FOURTH GRADE

10 BY DEFINITION, WHAT METRIC UNIT OF MEASUREMENT IS EQUAL TO ONE-THOUSANDTH OF A METER?

11 TRUE OR FALSE? 4 SQUARE FEET IS A LARGER AREA THAN 400 SQUARE INCHES.

12 IF JAMIR HAS 3 BOOKS THAT EACH WEIGH 2 POUNDS, 7 OUNCES, HOW MANY TOTAL OUNCES DO THEY WEIGH?

FIFTH GRADE

13 WHAT IS $14^{10}/_{14} - 9^{3}/_{7}$?

14 IT TAKES 7 GALLONS, 1 QUART OF PAINT TO PAINT YOUR HOUSE. YOU HAVE 4 GALLONS, 3 QUARTS. HOW MUCH MORE PAINT DO YOU NEED?

15 PATRICK DRANK 12 CUPS OF PUNCH AT THE SCHOOL DANCE. TO THE NEAREST WHOLE NUMBER, HOW MANY US LITERS DID HE DRINK?

FIRST GRADE

1 If Tristan and Mia each have a pair of pet parakeets, and their sister Sarah has a partridge, how many birds do the 3 siblings have in total?

2 How many whole numbers are there between 2 and 12, including 2 and 12?

3 Amira is measuring a table with a ruler. Which of these won't she be able to measure?

    a. the table's length
    b. the table's width
    c. the table's weight

SECOND GRADE

4 If you found 4 current US coins under the couch cushion and they added up to 25 cents, 3 of the coins must be what denomination?

5 Quinne has 26 cents' worth of change in her pockets. All the coins are identical. What kind of coin does she have?

6 On Tuesday Isabella eats half a pumpkin pie. If the next day she eats half of what's left over, what fraction of pie then remains?

THIRD GRADE

7 In a standard 12 by 12 multiplication table, what is the highest number listed on the table?

8 In the number 36.57921, what digit is in the thousandths place?

9 A decagon has how many sides?

FOURTH GRADE

10 If the radius of a circle is ¹/pi, what is the circumference of that circle?

11 What numbers make up the intersection of the set (3, 4, 5, 6) and the set (0, 2, 4, 6)?

12 What word is the plural of the mathematical term "radius"?

FIFTH GRADE

13 Parallel or perpendicular: Which type of lines intersect?

14 TRUE OR FALSE? 2 is the greatest common factor of 8 and 36.

15 By definition, "a bushel and a peck" is equivalent to how many gallons?

FIRST GRADE

1 **TRUE OR FALSE?** There are some numbers that have a 10 in the ones place.

2 If a standard clock reads 5:35 p.m., the minute hand is pointing to what number?

3 **TRUE OR FALSE?** The number 103 has a zero in the tens place.

SECOND GRADE

4 How many months of the year have 31 days?

5 If the month of April begins on a Thursday, it will end on what day of the week?

6 Quinne, Chloe, and Saya have a bowl with 18 tater tots. In order to share equally, how many tots should each get?

THIRD GRADE

7 If Colin's photo album has 6 photos per page, on what page is the 45th photo?

8 If Patrick can whittle 40 whistles in an hour, how many whistles can he whittle in 15 minutes?

9 If a magician pulled handkerchiefs out of his sleeve in the repeated order 1 red, 1 blue, 1 yellow, what color would the fourteenth handkerchief be?

FOURTH GRADE

10 The number 100 has a total of how many different positive factors?

11 If you multiply a three-digit whole number by another three-digit whole number, the product will have a minimum of how many digits?

12 The fraction ¹/₁₆ is equal to what percent?

FIFTH GRADE

13 Prime or post: What does the "p" stand for in the time "2:00 p.m."?

14 Isosceles or scalene: Which triangle has zero congruent sides?

15 What is the mode in the following set of numbers? 3, 4, 4, 5, 6, 7, 8

FIRST GRADE

1 TRUE OR FALSE? Some triangles have 4 sides.

2 If Nick divides a pie into quarters and eats 1 slice, how many slices are left?

3 If it's midnight on a standard clock, the minute hand is on what number?

SECOND GRADE

4 Which of the following is not a mathematical operation?

    a. division
    b. integer
    c. subtraction

5 If 6 dogs each buried 4 bones, what is the total number of bones that were buried?

6 If Jamir bought a handful of gummy worms for 78 cents and paid with 6 nickels, 4 dimes, and 1 quarter, how much change did he get back?

THIRD GRADE

7 If Tristan has 8 hot dogs and eats 6/16 of them, how many will he have left over?

8 Patrick's family is moving. If the truck can carry 10,000 pounds at a time, what is the maximum number of 50-pound boxes it can hold?

9 The lowest number in a set of numbers is 2. If the range of the set is 6, what is the highest number?

FOURTH GRADE

10 The quotient of 235/5 has what digit in the ones place?

11 What is the smallest positive integer that is both a composite number and a perfect square?

12 If you multiply a three-digit integer by another three-digit integer, the product will have a maximum of how many digits?

FIFTH GRADE

13 What's the volume of a right cylinder that has a base of 12 square inches and a height of 6 inches?

14 Which of the following is another way to express the number 5?

    a. $15/3$
    b. $20/5$
    c. $32/7$

15 A rhombus has 4 sides. How many of them are of equal length?

FIRST GRADE

1 If it's 11:00 a.m. right now, what time will it be in 7½ hours?

2 If Mia plays video games from midnight on Tuesday to midnight on Thursday, for how many hours has she played video games?

3 What is the sum of all the odd numbers between 2 and 20?

SECOND GRADE

5 If a US ton equals 2,000 pounds, how many combined pounds do a 2-ton baby hippo and his 4-ton mama weigh?

4 If Nick earns $2.00 an hour for every hour he spends raking leaves, and he works a total of 2½ hours, how much money has he earned?

6 If Quinne eats 3 doughnuts every morning, how many doughnuts will she have eaten in 4 days?

THIRD GRADE

7 If Chloe took a nap from 7:15 p.m. until 8:40 p.m., how many minutes did she sleep?

8 If 5 students each sent 12 text messages to Cooper, but 3 didn't go through, how many total messages did he receive?

FOURTH GRADE

9 What is the name of a rectangular prism in which all the sides are squares?

10 What are the only 2 numbers used in a traditional binary number system?

11 Jamir went on vacation and was gone for exactly 1 week. What is the total number of hours he was away?

12 What is the product of the third multiple of 3 and the fourth multiple of 4?

FIFTH GRADE

13 How many cups are in 5 US liquid quarts?

14 If y = 3x, and 3x = 12, then what number does y equal?

15 A pentagonal prism has how many total faces?

FIRST GRADE

1 TRUE OR FALSE? 1 DAY IS EQUIVALENT TO 12 HOURS.

2 TRUE OR FALSE? 4 + 15 EQUALS THE SAME NUMBER AS 15 + 4.

3 ON A CLOCK FACE, WHAT NUMBER IS THE BIG HAND ON IF THE TIME IS EXACTLY HALF PAST 2?

SECOND GRADE

4 IF TRISTAN PLAYED A VIDEO GAME FROM 11:45 A.M. UNTIL 3:15 P.M., PRECISELY HOW MANY HOURS AND MINUTES WAS HE GAMING?

5 WHICH OF THE FIRST 5 WHOLE NUMBERS HAS THE MOST LETTERS WHEN WRITTEN IN ROMAN NUMERALS?

6 JAMIR THREW HIS PAPER AIRPLANE 134 INCHES, ISABELLA THREW HERS 4 YARDS, AND CHLOE THREW HER PLANE 10 FEET. WHO THREW THEIR PLANE THE FARTHEST?

THIRD GRADE

7 SAYA, MIA, AND COLIN EQUALLY SHARE 1,242 GUMBALLS. HOW MANY DOES EACH KID GET?

8 IF ISABELLA GETS PAID $5 EVERY TIME SHE TUTORS HER BROTHER, HOW MANY DOLLARS WOULD SHE HAVE AFTER TUTORING HIM EVERY DAY IN JULY?

9 ELEMENTARY SCHOOL STUDENTS SOLD THEIR USED BOOKS TO RAISE MONEY FOR CHARITY. IF 30 BOOKS WERE SOLD FOR $5.50 EACH, HOW MUCH MONEY DID THEY RAISE?

10 QUINNE RODE HER BICYCLE 19 MILES ON SATURDAY AND 17 MILES ON SUNDAY. SHE BIKED A TOTAL OF 4 HOURS. HOW MANY MILES PER HOUR DID SHE AVERAGE?

11 WHAT UNIT OF MEASUREMENT WAS ORIGINALLY CREATED BY THE ROMANS TO DESCRIBE THE DISTANCE COVERED BY 1,000 PACES OF A SOLDIER?

12 TWO INTEGERS HAVE AN ABSOLUTE VALUE OF 3. ONE OF THOSE INTEGERS IS 3. WHAT IS THE OTHER?

FIFTH GRADE

13 MEASURED IN DEGREES, WHAT IS THE SMALLEST OBTUSE ANGLE THAT IS A WHOLE NUMBER?

14 WHAT IS THE SUM OF THE DEGREES OF THE INTERIOR ANGLES OF AN OCTAGON?

15 HOW MANY WATTS ARE IN A GIGAWATT?

FIRST GRADE

1 If a dozen birds are flying to Florida from Virginia and a dozen join them in Georgia, how many dozens of birds have flocked together in flight?

2 If the clock is set at 8:00 a.m. and the teacher moves the hour hand 3 hours clockwise, what time does it read now?

3 What is the next number in the following sequence? 2, 5, 9, 14, ___

SECOND GRADE

4 How many seconds are in 3½ minutes?

    a. 102
    b. 210
    c. 311

5 **TRUE OR FALSE?** If the temperature is 10 degrees below zero Fahrenheit and it rises 40 degrees, it is still below freezing.

6 If a brick is 5 inches long and a wall is 9 bricks long, how many inches long is that wall?

THIRD GRADE

7 50 people were asked to name their favorite season. 16 said summer, 12 said fall, and 15 said spring. How many said winter?

8 What is the missing number in the equation: 72 ÷ ____ = 9

9 How many decades are in 14 millennia?

FOURTH GRADE

10 What is the answer to this math problem? 6 + (12 − 6) / 2

11 The sum of all angles on any triangle is how many degrees?

12 If a number set is referred to as a "null set," how many members does it have?

FIFTH GRADE

13 A cube has how many straight edges?

14 What number is the next perfect square after 49?

15 In billions, what is the difference of 1.3 trillion and 1.1 trillion?

FIRST GRADE

1 A day and a half is equivalent to how many hours?

2 What is the sum of the even whole numbers between 11 and 17?

3 Jamir has 5 apples. Patrick eats 3 of them, and Mia takes 2 others. How many apples does Jamir have left?

SECOND GRADE

4 If Cooper saves a dime from his lunch money every day, how many dollars will he have in 20 days?

5 If Tristan is facing north and turns 90 degrees to his right, what direction is he now facing?

6 Round the number 350 to the nearest hundred.

7 If Colin bench-pressed 60 pounds the first week, then doubled the weight every week, how many pounds would he lift in the fourth week?

THIRD GRADE

8 What prime number is a factor of 289?

9 A hexagon has how many more sides than a quadrilateral?

FOURTH GRADE

11 Mia is building a wood frame for an 8-inch × 10-inch picture. Exactly how many feet of wood does she need to make the frame?

10 If you take the square root of 16 and add it to the square root of 9, the answer you get is the square root of what other number?

12 If Isabella travels in a high-speed train moving at 520 miles an hour for 3½ hours, how many miles has she traveled?

FIFTH GRADE

13 24 pints of paint is equal to how many gallons?

14 How is the year 2022 expressed in Roman numerals?

15 In standard US measurements, how many miles are in a league?

FIRST GRADE

1 What is 27 rounded to the nearest 10?

SECOND GRADE

4 Which of the following can replace the blank to make the equation correct? 26 + 49 _ 21 + 54

    a. <
    b. >
    c. =

THIRD GRADE

7 A polygon has a minimum of how many sides?

8 How many of the interior angles in a scalene triangle have the same number of degrees?

9 If you ate 2 peanut butter and jelly sandwiches every day for 365 days, how many sandwiches is that?

2 If a class of 14 students separates evenly into 2 mathlete teams, how many students are there per team?

3 **TRUE OR FALSE?** If during a given year, December 3 falls on a Monday, then December 12 will be on a Friday.

5 Amira wants to collect 150 cans of food for her food drive. If she collects 23 cans from the glee club and 46 cans from the football team, how many does she still need?

6 Cooper is 53 inches tall. Tristan is 2 inches taller than Saya. Saya is 3 inches shorter than Cooper. How tall is Tristan?

FOURTH GRADE

10 If LeBron James scored 400 points over the course of 10 NBA regulation games, how many points did he average per quarter?

11 If your mom sends you to the store for 3 gallons of ice cream but the store only sells pints, how many pints should you buy?

12 How many total degrees are there if you add up the interior angles in an equilateral triangle?

FIFTH GRADE

13 Patrick took a test that had 200 questions, and he got 88% of them correct. How many questions did he answer incorrectly?

14 What is the product of the first 2 prime numbers?

15 What is 10 to the ninth power plus 10 to the eighth power?

FIRST GRADE

1
If you have 2 roses and 3 lilies but give away 4 flowers, how many flowers do you now have?

2
What is the sum of the even whole numbers between 7 and 11?

3
If Colin has 6 grapes and Quinne takes a third of them, how many grapes does Colin have left?

SECOND GRADE

4
Chloe lives in Oregon. Her friend lives in Vermont. If Chloe wants to web chat with her friend at 6:00 p.m. PST, what time will it be in Vermont?

5
Mia shot 5 arrows in archery class. If 3 arrows hit the 20-point circle and 2 arrows hit the 50-point bull's-eye, how many points did Mia score?

6
In terms of volume, which of the following is the largest?
- a. a cup of juice
- b. a pint of juice
- c. a quart of juice

THIRD GRADE

7 Which numbers are the addends in the following equation?
$7 \times 1 = 3 + 4$

8 If a T-shirt cannon shoots 3 shirts in a shot, how many shots does it take to shoot 17 shirts?

9 What is $14^{10}/_{14} - 9^{3}/_{7}$?

FOURTH GRADE

10 Between 1 and 100, how many multiples of 9 are odd numbers?

11 Which of these numbers is the largest?
a. $^{17}/_5$
b. $^{19}/_6$
c. $^{22}/_7$

12 Dividing $^{7}/_3$ by $^{4}/_9$ gives you the same number as multiplying $^{7}/_3$ by the simplest form of what improper fraction?

FIFTH GRADE

13 If Isabella read 25% of her 80 e-mails, how many does she still have left to read?

14 What is the second digit after the decimal point when writing pi numerically?

15 What is the measure, in degrees, of a straight angle?

FIRST GRADE

1. IF YOU HAVE 2½ PAIRS OF SHOES, HOW MANY SHOES DO YOU HAVE?

2. TRUE OR FALSE? ON LINES NUMBERED 1 THROUGH 10, LINE 6 IS 4 AWAY FROM LINE 10.

3. WHICH OF THE FOLLOWING IS NOT A TOOL DESIGNED TO WEIGH OBJECTS?
   A. BALANCE   B. SCALE   C. RULER

SECOND GRADE

4. IF NICK CAN PEEL 10 POTATOES IN AN HOUR, AND QUINNE CAN PEEL 10 POTATOES IN 2 HOURS, HOW MANY POTATOES CAN THEY PEEL IN AN HOUR WORKING TOGETHER?

5. TRUE OR FALSE? $1 \times 1 = 1 + 1$.

6. IN US CURRENCY, 25 CENTS ARE EQUAL TO WHAT FRACTION OF $1?

THIRD GRADE

7. IF 1 ROLL OF TOILET PAPER IS 350 FEET LONG, HOW MANY FEET ARE IN 6 ROLLS OF TOILET PAPER?

8. IF A ROCKET TRAVELS AT A CONSTANT RATE OF 6 FEET PER SECOND, HOW MANY SECONDS WOULD IT TAKE FOR THE ROCKET TO TRAVEL 102 FEET?

9. HOW MANY RIGHT ANGLES ARE IN A SQUARE?

FOURTH GRADE

10 WHICH OF THESE IS A SUFFIX OF AN ORDINAL NUMBER?
    A. ETH   B. RD   C. SH

11 WHICH OF THESE IS A UNIT USED FOR MEASURING DEPTH?
    A. KNOTS   B. FATHOMS   C. MACH

12 IF JAMIR'S PET RABBIT HAS A LITTER OF 8 BABIES, AND EACH OF THOSE BABIES GROWS UP AND HAS A LITTER OF 8 BABIES, HOW MANY TOTAL RABBITS WILL JAMIR HAVE?

FIFTH GRADE

13 COOPER AND PATRICK CHIP IN TO BUY A SKATEBOARD FOR $100.00. IF THERE'S AN 8.25% TAX ON IT, HOW MUCH IS THE TOTAL COST?

14 HOW MANY TOTAL MINUTES ARE THERE IN 365 DAYS?

15 WHAT IS THE SUM OF THE FIRST 2 PRIME NUMBERS?

FIRST GRADE

1 If the clock currently reads 2:43 p.m., how many minutes is it until 3:00 p.m.?

2 If 7 children send 4 text messages, how many text messages total do they send?

    a. 28 b. 48 c. 14

3 How many odd numbers are between 0 and 10?

    a. 3 b. 5 c. 7

SECOND GRADE

4 If 3 identical blocks laid end to end total 1 foot in length, then how many inches long is 1 of those blocks?

5 If a town has an average monthly rainfall of 1 inch, what is the total number of inches of rainfall it receives in 1 year, on average?

6 How many right angles does a rectangle have?

THIRD GRADE

7 On a clock face, which makes the most revolutions?

    a. the little hand in 20 days

    b. the big hand in 2 days

    c. the seconds hand in 30 minutes

8 Which number comes next in the following sequence? 81, 63, 45, 27, 32, 18, __?

9 What do you determine by multiplying an object's length, width, and height?

a. mass
b. density
c. volume

FOURTH GRADE

10 If a quadrilateral has angles of 30, 40, and 112 degrees, how many degrees is the fourth angle?

11 What is the maximum number of angles formed by the intersection of 2 lines?

12 If Amira sells lemonade for 40 cents a glass and she spent $7 making the lemonade, how many glasses does she need to sell to make a profit?

FIFTH GRADE

13 How many square inches are there in a square foot?

14 What is the greatest common factor of 2 and 3?

15 If the average of 13, 19, and k is 17, what is the value of k?

FIRST GRADE

1 Which unit of measurement is most often used when measuring the weight of a cargo ship?
a. gallons
b. yards
c. tons

2 Which is a metric unit for measuring volume?
a. liter
b. quart
c. buttload

3 TRUE OR FALSE?
It is possible to divide a square into 2 triangles.

SECOND GRADE

4 How much is 2 divided by 2?

5 How many mathematical operations are in the following equation?
$7 \times (12 - 8) = 28$
a. 0
b. 1
c. 2

6 What is the largest positive single-digit integer Jane can add to 2 and still have a positive single-digit integer as the result?

THIRD GRADE

7 TRUE OR FALSE?
A composite number can be prime.

8 TRUE OR FALSE?
A rectangle has more right angles than a square.

9 Tristan began soccer practice at 1:05 p.m. and played for 1 hour and 35 minutes. It then took him 45 minutes to walk to his house. At what time did he get home?

FOURTH GRADE

10 Which of the first 4 whole numbers does not divide evenly into 4?

11 How many vertices does a cylinder have?

12 In US measurements, how many zeros do you need to add to 1 million to make it into 1 quadrillion?

FIFTH GRADE

13 How many ounces are in a typical US ton?

14 How many total days are there in June, July, and August?

15 What is the additive inverse of 12?

FIRST GRADE

1 If yesterday was Wednesday, what day of the week is tomorrow?

    a. Friday
    b. Monday
    c. ice cream sundae

2 Which is a better estimate for the weight of a regulation-size soccer ball?

    a. 16 ounces
    b. 16 pounds
    c. 16 tons

3 The number 10 is composed of two digits. Zero is one of the digits. What is the other?

SECOND GRADE

4 In the answer to the equation 23 + 12, what number is in the tens place?

5 TRUE OR FALSE? Up and down are cardinal directions.

6 How many odd-numbered days are in the month of February during a non-leap year?

THIRD GRADE

7 If 1 inch represents 9 miles on a map, how many miles would 7 inches indicate?

8 If it is 10:00 a.m. in Salt Lake City, Utah, what time is it in Cleveland, Ohio?

9 If you were to travel at the speed of light, how long would it take for you to travel 5 light-years?

FOURTH GRADE

10 What is 3¾ written as an improper fraction?

11 Patrick has a scale map where 1 inch equals 10 miles. If the distance on the map from his house to his school is ¾ inch, how many miles away is the school?

12 To convert Fahrenheit to Celsius, you take ⁹⁄₅ of the Celsius temperature and then add what number?

FIFTH GRADE

13 If $x - y = 2y$ and $x = 9$, what is the value of y?

14 Five friends equally share a gluten-free vegan pie. What percentage of the pie does each friend get?

15 Rounded to the nearest whole number, what is the area of a circle that has a radius of 10?

FIRST GRADE

1 If Saya dances for ¾ of an hour, what is the total number of minutes that she is dancing?

2 What is the smallest whole number greater than 1?

3 Your class has 17 students. If 6 new students join the class, what is the total number of students in the class?

SECOND GRADE

4 Tristan found worms in ⅕ of his apple pie. What percentage of his pie had worms in it?

5 If the maximum number of friends Cooper is allowed to have at his birthday party is 28, how many sets of quintuplets could he invite?

6 **TRUE OR FALSE?** On a number line, the number 16 is closer to 10 than to 20.

THIRD GRADE

7 Isabella brings 3 dozen doughnuts to class. Nick, Jamir, and Chloe have 3 doughnuts each. How many doughnuts are left?

8 Which is longer: 14 yards or 40 feet?

9 Chloe's cat has 5 black kittens, 2 white kittens, and 3 gray kittens. If she picks 1 up at random, what is the probability it will be a gray kitten?

FOURTH GRADE

10 What is .16 written as a fraction in lowest terms?

11 In square inches, what is the surface area of a cube with 5-inch sides?

12 Jamir competed in a triathlon that is ½ cycling, ¼ swimming, and ¼ running. If he ran for 3 miles, how many miles long was the entire race?

FIFTH GRADE

13 What is the square root of the square root of 256?

14 In the following equation, what number must n be to make the fractions equivalent? $4/13 = 24/n$

15 What is the surface area in square feet of a rectangular solid with dimensions 3 feet, 3 feet, and 4 feet?

51

FIRST GRADE

1. WHICH OF THESE PHRASES IS THE BEST WAY TO HELP REMEMBER THE DIRECTIONS ON A TYPICAL COMPASS WHEN READING THEM CLOCKWISE?
   - A. WOMBATS EAT NOODLE SOUP
   - B. NOBODY ENJOYS WALLABY SARCASM
   - C. NARWHALS EASILY SPEAK WEASELESE

2. IF YOU HAVE 3 CURRENT US COINS THAT ADD UP TO 21 CENTS, 2 OF THE COINS ARE WHAT?
   - A. PENNIES   B. NICKELS
   - C. DIMES

3. TRUE OR FALSE? IF JILL HAS 4 PICKLES AND CUTS EACH ONE INTO QUARTERS, SHE NOW HAS A TOTAL OF 16 PICKLE PIECES.

SECOND GRADE

4. IF WE BUILD A RECTANGULAR RACETRACK WITH SIDES OF 20 FEET AND 30 FEET, WHAT IS ITS PERIMETER?

5. IF OCTOBER 1 FALLS ON A TUESDAY, WHAT DAY OF THE WEEK WILL HALLOWEEN FALL ON?

6. IF A CAR'S ENGINE IS TURNING AT 10,000 REVOLUTIONS PER MINUTE, HOW MANY REVOLUTIONS PER HOUR IS THAT?

THIRD GRADE

7. IF THE PERIMETER OF A SQUARE IS 28, WHAT IS THE LENGTH OF ONE OF ITS SIDES?

8. IF YOU DIVIDE 84 BY 5, WHAT IS THE REMAINDER?

9. A QUART PLUS A GALLON EQUALS HOW MANY TOTAL QUARTS?

FOURTH GRADE

10. WHAT'S THE DATE IF YOU'RE CELEBRATING ALBERT EINSTEIN'S BIRTHDAY BY EATING PIE ON PI DAY?

11. ON A NUMBER LINE DIVIDED INTO TENTHS, HOW MANY SPACES SEPARATE 6.1 FROM 8.3?

12. WHAT IS THE HIGHEST TWO-DIGIT NUMBER THAT IS NOT A PALINDROME?

FIFTH GRADE

13. HOW MANY FACES ARE ON A DODECAHEDRON?

14. HOW MANY CUPS ARE IN 28 FLUID OUNCES?

15. HOW MANY MICROMETERS ARE IN ONE CENTIMETER?

FIRST GRADE

1 **TRUE OR FALSE?** 11 is the second-lowest two-digit counting number.

SECOND GRADE

4 $\frac{1}{10}$ is to 10% as ¼ is to what percent?

5 What is the minimum number of current US coins Mia needs to make exactly 37 cents?

THIRD GRADE

7 How much is 10 billion divided by 10 million?

8 In math class, 3 students got a score of 100, 2 students got a score of 92, and 4 students got a score of 88. What score was the mode?

2 If a class of 16 students splits evenly into two separate teams for a game of dodgeball at recess, how many students are there per team?

3 Saya's party started at 7:00 p.m. and ended at 10:00 p.m. What was the total number of minutes that Saya's party lasted?

6 Nick bought two hamburgers for a total of $3.14. If he paid with a $5 bill, how much change will he get?

9 If Isabella's pet cockroach is 1 inch long, approximately how many millimeters long is it?

   a. 25
   b. 250
   c. 2,500

FOURTH GRADE

10 How many factors does the number 51 have?

11 If 11 divided by *k* has a remainder of 5, what is 2*k*?

12 **TRUE OR FALSE?** No prime number greater than 5 ends in a 5.

FIFTH GRADE

13 Chloe has 5 more wrestling cards than Colin. If together they have 23 cards, how many cards does Colin have?

14 A cube has a volume of 8 cubic inches. What is its surface area in square inches?

15 For an isosceles triangle whose interior angles are all positive integers, what is the greatest number of degrees a single interior angle can be?

ANSWER KEY

PAGES 8-9:
FIRST GRADE

1. tray 1
2. 12
3. x
4. 7
5. false
6. b
7. b
8. 40
9. 30
10. b
11. 7
12. 21

PAGES 10-11:
SECOND GRADE

1. 9 inches
2. true
3. 2
4. 6
5. 30 inches
6. c
7. 1 hour and 45 minutes
8. 4
9. 2
10. b
11. 2
12. 9

PAGES 12-13:
THIRD GRADE

1. 20 degrees Celsius
2. true
3. 40 weeks
4. 3 feet
5. c
6. $38
7. 9
8. $2.00
9. b
10. false
11. 0
12. true

PAGES 14-15:
FOURTH GRADE

1. 2
2. true
3. 6 hours and 40 minutes (also accept: 400 minutes, 6⅔ hours)
4. 212 degrees
5. 4 pounds
6. 9
7. 12.5%
8. 8
9. 0
10. 4
11. 8
12. XX

PAGES 16-17:
FIFTH GRADE

1. 4
2. 40%
3. 40
4. $7.50
5. 10,000
6. 2
7. 5
8. 10,560 ft
9. 1
10. 20
11. 10,000
12. 640

PAGES 20-21:

1. 15
2. 2
3. true
4. false
5. b
6. 126 inches
7. 6
8. 2.5
9. 2
10. 20
11. 0
12. $^{25}/_{33}$
13. 4,840
14. 64 cm cubed
15. 2

PAGES 22-23:

1. 10
2. addition
3. Mia
4. December 30
5. 53 minutes
6. 932
7. false
8. 7
9. 24
10. millimeter
11. true
12. 117 ounces

13. $5\frac{2}{7}$ (also accept: $5\frac{4}{14}$)
14. 10 quarts
15. 3

PAGES 24-25:

1. 5
2. 11
3. c
4. nickels
5. penny
6. ¼
7. 144
8. 9
9. 10
10. 2
11. 4 and 6
12. radii
13. perpendicular
14. false
15. 10

PAGES 26-27:

1. false
2. 7
3. true
4. 7 (January, March, May, July, August, October, December)
5. Friday
6. 6
7. 8th page
8. 10 whistles
9. blue
10. 9
11. 5
12. 6.25%
13. post
14. scalene
15. 4

PAGES 28-29:

1. false
2. 3
3. 12
4. b
5. 24
6. 17 cents
7. 5
8. 200
9. 8
10. 7
11. 4
12. 6
13. 72 (cubic inches)
14. a
15. 4

PAGES 30-31:

1. 6:30 p.m. (also accept: 1830)
2. 48
3. 99
4. $5
5. 12,000
6. 12
7. 85 minutes
8. 57
9. cube
10. 0 and 1
11. 168
12. 144
13. 20 cups
14. 12
15. 7

PAGES 32-33:

1. false
2. true
3. 6
4. 3 hours and 30 minutes
5. 3
6. Isabella
7. 414
8. $155

9. $165
10. 9
11. mile
12. negative three (also accept: minus three)
13. 91
14. 1,080
15. 1 billon

PAGES 34-35:

1. 2
2. 11:00 a.m.
3. 20
4. b
5. true
6. 45 inches
7. 7
8. 8
9. 1,400
10. 9
11. 180
12. 0
13. 12
14. 64
15. 200 billion

PAGES 36-37:

1. 36
2. 42
3. 0
4. $2.00
5. east
6. 400
7. 480
8. 17
9. 2
10. 49
11. 3 feet
12. 1,820 miles
13. 3 gallons
14. MMXXII
15. 3

PAGES 38-39:

1. 30
2. 7
3. false
4. c
5. 81
6. 52 inches
7. 3
8. 0
9. 730
10. 10
11. 24
12. 180
13. 24
14. 6
15. 1,100,000,000 (also accept: 1.1 billion)

PAGES 40-41:

1. 1
2. 18
3. 4
4. 9:00 p.m.
5. 160
6. c
7. 3 and 4
8. 6
9. 5 2/7
10. 6
11. a
12. 9/4
13. 60
14. 4
15. 180

PAGES 42-43:

1. 5
2. true
3. c
4. 15
5. false
6. ¼ (also accept: one-quarter)
7. 2,100

8. 17
9. 4
10. b
11. b
12. 73
13. $108.25
14. 525,600
15. 5

PAGES 44-45:

1. 17 minutes
2. a
3. b
4. 4 inches
5. 12 inches
6. 4
7. b
8. 27
9. c
10. 178
11. 4
12. 18
13. 144
14. 1
15. 19

PAGES 46-47:

1. c
2. a
3. true
4. 1
5. c
6. 7
7. false
8. false
9. 3:25 p.m.
10. 3
11. 0
12. 9
13. 32,000
14. 92
15. negative 12

PAGES 48-49:

1. a
2. a
3. 1
4. 3
5. false
6. 14
7. 63
8. 12:00 p.m.
9. 5 years (also accept: 5 Earth years; do not accept: 5 light-years)
10. 15/4
11. 7.5 miles
12. 32
13. 3
14. 20%
15. 314

PAGES 50-51:

1. 45 minutes
2. 2
3. 23
4. 20%
5. 5
6. false
7. 27
8. 14 yards
9. 3/10 (also accept: 30%)
10. 4/25
11. 150 square inches
12. 12 miles
13. 4
14. 78
15. 66 square feet

PAGES 52-53:

1. c
2. c
3. true
4. 100 feet
5. Thursday

6. 600,000
7. 7
8. 4
9. 5 quarts
10. March 14
11. 22
12. 98
13. 12
14. 3.5
15. 10,000

PAGES 54-55:

1. true
2. 8
3. 180 minutes
4. 25%
5. 4
6. $1.86
7. 1,000
8. 88

9. a
10. 4
11. 12
12. true
13. 9
14. 24 square inches
15. 178

PHOTO CREDITS

PENGUIN YOUNG READERS LICENSES
An Imprint of Penguin Random House LLC, New York

MGM

Published in 2020 by Penguin Young Readers Licenses, an imprint of Penguin Random House LLC, New York. Manufactured in China.

Visit us online at www.penguinrandomhouse.com.

ISBN 9780593222386   10 9 8 7 6 5 4 3 2 1